MINDFULNESS

Edited by
Tiddy Rowan

quadrille

When you are on a journey, it is certainly helpful to know where you're going – but remember: the only thing that is ultimately real about your journey is the step that you are taking at this moment. That's all there ever is.

At first, mindfulness can seem like an intangible concept. However, practising mindfulness is, quite simply, the act of concentrating on your breathing, being aware of your breath and being aware of what is going on around you in the present moment. The more you do it, the more the simplicity of it becomes clear and the benefits manifold. It lightens the mind and the spirit.

" Mindfulness is a very simple form of meditation that was little known in the West until recently. A typical meditation consists of focusing your full attention on your breath as it flows in and out of your body. Focusing on each breath in this way allows you to observe your thoughts as they arise in your mind and, little by little, to let go of struggling with them. "

PROFESSOR MARK WILLIAMS

Focusing your thoughts.

- Do you tend to get so focused on the goal that you want to achieve that you lose touch with what you are doing right now to get there?

- Do you then rush through activities without being really attentive, to the point that you never quite reach that goal?

Practising mindfulness, creating a mental environment that is harmonious and peaceful, is conducive to clarity of thought.

The essence of the discipline is in the word – mindfulness – being mindful.

Being aware with real attention. Strengthen this muscle again and again by using breathing as a constant access, whenever you want or need it.

It is easy to read about the importance of being mindful and then forget about it and not actually apply it. Mindfulness, and all its benefits, will not become apparent until you've really engaged with it. And like everything, it gets better with practice. Even the first time you do the simple breathing technique, really take time out (and we're only talking about a few minutes initially) to experience it for yourself – the result is immediate. It will empower and encourage you to take another step and then another, until you are being mindful in other activities.

Opening this book at any page will hopefully give you a recipe to remind you of the importance of staying (or more likely returning to) the here and now. Each time you engage with a mindfulness notice and link it to an increasing number of daily activities you reinforce the whole concept.

As you develop this practice it will come to you naturally and you will reap all the benefits. Your spark will return, you will find new enjoyment in simple activities, you will not yearn or crave for something in the future or mourn the undone past, and you will be more relaxed and yet mentally more alert and enthusiastic. Your relationships and communications with people will change. In short this is a pivotal moment – right now as you're reading these words – to improving and brightening your whole life and outlook.

" *If you try to calm [the mind], it only makes it worse, but over time it does calm, and when it does, there's room to hear more subtle things – that's when your intuition starts to blossom and you start to see things more clearly and be in the present more. Your mind just slows down, and you see a tremendous expanse in the moment. You see so much more than you could see before. It's a discipline, you have to practise it.* "

STEVE JOBS

People assume that mindfulness is part of Buddhist teaching. Although many of the exercises and techniques are rooted in Buddhism, the practice can be taught for secular (or mixed) groups or individuals. A basic understanding of Buddhism or Zen principles might be helpful in understanding mindfulness (and vice versa) but the two are by no means interdependent. Whether in a 'secular' or 'spiritual context', mindfulness alleviates suffering and increases our awareness in ways that can only be a gain.

Breathing to relax.

A deeply relaxed person breathes around seven times a minute. Slow your breathing right down and you will automatically relax.

This is especially helpful when you need to focus, do a presentation, attend an interview or simply just to calm down.

1. Breathe in (count to 6 – approximately)

2. Hold it (count to 2)

3. Let the breath out slowly (count to 8 – approximately)

" We are not human beings having a spiritual experience. We are spiritual beings having a human experience."

PIERRE TEILHARD DE CHARDIN

" Mindfulness meditation, especially when it is understood as being a way of living life as if it really mattered, moment by moment, rather than merely as a technique ... is one powerful vehicle for realising such transformative and healing possibilities. "

JON KABAT-ZINN

Be non-judgemental in your own thoughts, feelings and beliefs.

It is important sometimes to let things be, just as they are, and allow them to breathe without questioning or fixing them.

" *Worldly fools search for exotic masters, not realising that their own mind is the master.* "

BODHIDHARMA

Be mindful of how you behave towards other people.

Particularly in conversation – concentrate on listening and engaging rather than letting your mind wander or thinking ahead to what you are going to say next.

Stay in the moment.

You'll be amazed by how much better the communication will be.

" Let go of your mind and then be mindful. Close your ears and listen! "

RUMI

**Listen to your inner voice –
allow it to be heard.**

Remember to trust yourself. Your intuition
and abilities are the natural building blocks
of handling developments.

Under pressure or in a crisis we act
instinctively. Let these instincts have a role
in whatever you undertake or decide in your
daily activities.

The UK National Institute of Clinical Excellence (NICE) has endorsed Mindfulness Based Cognitive Therapy (MBCT) as an effective treatment for depression and the prevention of depression relapse. Research has shown that people who have been clinically depressed three or more times (sometimes for 20 years or more) find that taking the programme and learning these skills helps to reduce considerably their chances that depression will return.

www.mbct.co.uk

Mindfulness is central to a methodology in courses treating depression known as MBCT (Mindfulness Based Cognitive Therapy). But mindfulness is not only about getting out of a bad place, it is just as much about staying in, or getting to, a good place.

People can benefit from mindfulness whether they have a specific problem or not ... Developing greater awareness can open us to seeing how the mind becomes entangled in and blinded by its own liking and disliking, pursuing and rejecting when we try to maximise our happiness. Mindfulness helps us see with greater clarity how we may approach our moment-by-moment experience skilfully, taking more pleasure in the good things that often go unnoticed or unappreciated, and dealing more effectively with the difficulties we encounter, both real and imagined.

www.mbct.co.uk

" Human beings, by changing the inner attitudes of their minds, can change the outer aspects of their lives. "

WILLIAM JAMES

Mindfulness cannot happen in the future, but only in the here and now.

It is found in the ordinary, the obvious, the mundane and the exotic.

All it means is bringing your attention and awareness to everything and everyone around you.

Reading this book, now.

Even as your mind starts wandering off to its next command, you can bring it back to the now by taking a breath and paying attention to it – unhurriedly – just as it is.

And take another breath just for good measure.

As you are doing that, your mind does not ruminate but allows you to concentrate on the task in hand.

As you increase your practice of mindfulness, you will find that you gradually stop labelling events and thoughts under emotional headings such as 'negative', 'irritating' and 'boring'.

You will develop a way of observing them and moving on.

Mindfulness has to be experienced, rather than described.

The best way in – like any endeavour – is just to start.

Simply start by being aware of your next three breaths.

" Until one is committed, there is hesitancy, the chance to draw back. Concerning all acts of initiative (and creation), there is one elementary truth, the ignorance of which kills countless ideas and splendid plans: that the moment one definitely commits oneself, then Providence moves too. [This raises] in one's favour all manner of unforeseen incidents and meetings and material assistance, which no man could have dreamed would have come his way. Whatever you can do, or dream you can do, begin it. Boldness has genius, power, and magic in it. Begin it now. "

W.H. MURRAY

Go for a walk.

Walking is one of the finest forms of exercise, a proven stress reliever and mood booster and can be made doubly valuable by using it as a mindful exercise to be aware of everything around you – sights, sounds, colours and the weather. When your thoughts stray to concerns and worries, just guide your mind back to the exercise of being aware of your surroundings as you walk.

Don't wait to see what the weather is like – a walk in the wind or rain can be every bit as stimulating, sometimes more so, than a walk in the sunshine.

Take time out to pop in to an art gallery or museum.

Don't make it a special occasion; slot it into your day – any day.

1. Find one piece that attracts you and stay with that one item for 5, 10 or even 20 minutes.

2. Absorb it, enter into it.

3. Then leave the gallery.

When you are outside again you will feel refreshed, because your mind has not been chattering for a spell – it has left you in peace in order to focus on something else.

"Just to experience such sustained elemental stillness outwardly and the interior silence that can accompany it, is ample reason for arranging one's life to cultivate and bathe in this possibility from time to time."

JON KABAT-ZINN

**Mindfulness helps us to face our
self-conscious fears.**

It's hard to live in the moment if we worry
about what others might be thinking of us.
Self-consciousness sets up a dual thinking
process, so instead of listening to the other
person or concentrating on what we want or
need to say, we are also wondering how we are
coming across.

By practising mindfulness to be ourselves
and to be present, we will not only overcome
any self-conscious fears or worries about the
opinions others may have of us, but we will
become more relaxed and engaged.

Observing your thoughts.

This exercise is akin to meditation, but it is an exercise in mindfulness just the same. So don't be put off by the idea of 'meditating'. It is a very simple exercise, but very helpful in quieting an unruly mind and dispersing unwanted emotions.

1. Set aside a time when you know you won't be interrupted and switch off your phone.

2. Sit however is comfortable for you. It doesn't need to be cross-legged on the floor, a chair will do fine. But sit with a straight back (straight not rigid) and preferably without leaning against the back of the chair. The idea is to remain comfortable but attentive.

3. Close your eyes and observe your breathing just as it is. There's no need to change anything. Just watch and observe each breath coming in and going out.

4. Thoughts will try to get in and take your attention – don't let that concern you. Observe them. Let go of them and get back to focusing, once again, on your breathing.

5. Practise this exercise for just five minutes to begin with.

Practise at some point every day, increasing it to longer periods whenever possible.

That's all there is to it.

" Don't worry about what the world needs. Ask what makes you come alive and do that. Because what the world needs is people who have come alive. "

HOWARD THURMAN

**Riding out your emotions:
Worry surfing.**

Imagine for a moment an ocean wave as it approaches the shore. It's steep and tall and hasn't crested yet into a breaker. Now imagine the wave nearing a group of gulls floating on the water. The birds don't fly away. They simply ride up the facing slope, round the top and drift down the long back of the wave.

That's what you can learn to do with your worries, anxieties, and fears. All emotions are wave-like and time-limited. They ebb and flow. Life's a wave: emotions build up, eventually reach a peak, and drift away. Worries, anxieties and fears come and go in a similar way. They don't last forever, even if it feels like they will.

www.themindfulword.org

Do you find thoughts coming in to your mind at random as though you have no control over them? Do you get to your destination and cannot remember a simple function such as having locked the front door, turned off the iron etc? We tend to live so much of our lives on autopilot that it can feel as though our minds have a will of their own and that the thoughts that come to us are random. Mindfulness teaches us how not to let random thinking swamp us, but to observe it and then regain control over our own minds.

Identify a piece of jewellery that you wear – a pendant, a ring or a watch – to which you can attribute 'mindfulness'. Throughout the day when you look at it or touch it, let it be a prompt for you to bring yourself into the present moment.

Follow your breath in and out and return – within seconds – to what you were doing or talking about with renewed mindfulness.

The tendency is to react as if our emotions were a problem to be solved: we start trying to use our critical-thinking strategies. When these do not work, we redouble our efforts to use them. We end up overthinking, brooding, ruminating and living in our heads. This is where mindfulness can create a break in the current, stop the babble and calm everything down.

" What you resist, persists. "

CARL JUNG

The body scan.

Mindfulness courses all include a variation of this. It is a simple meditation to combine awareness of the sensations in the body and breath. It can be done for as briefly as five minutes if you like. You can begin at the top of your head and work down to the toes. Or start at the toes and work up. Whichever comes more naturally.

1. Lie down on your back somewhere comfortable and undisturbed.

2. Take a few moments to become aware of the physical sensations in your body.

3. Move your attention towards your breath and feel the stomach expanding on every inhalation and releasing on every exhalation.

4. Guide your attention to the top of the head and explore sensations in this part of the body.

5. Expand the attention to the back of the head, the sides of the head, the scalp, the forehead, the temples, the eyes and the face.

6. Let all the muscles of the face relax and fall into rest.

7. Move down to each area – the neck, the shoulders, the arms into the wrists, the hands and the tips of the fingers.

8. Back up to the shoulders and down the back, to the buttocks and pelvis.

9. To the front of the torso, the abdomen moving with the breath.

10. Let the whole body sink into whatever you're lying on.

11. Move your attention and breath down into the thighs, down the legs to the ankles, the feet and each of the toes.

12. Spread your attention back to the body as a whole, restful and relaxed.

13. Slowly start to move the fingers and toes, stretching the arms above the head and give the body a good stretch.

14. Gently roll over and come back up to sitting then standing to return to your daily activity with a renewed sense of awareness and energy.

Research has shown that mindfulness improves memory, creativity, and reaction times. It also boosts the immune system and lowers blood pressure. Studies have also shown that mindfulness can help with rheumatoid arthritis, chronic fatigue syndrome, and speech stuttering.

PROF. MARK WILLIAMS AND DR. DANNY PENMAN
Mindfulness: A practical guide to finding peace in a frantic world

Take a few moments to stop and notice whatever sounds are going on around you at this moment.

- It could be a car horn, people chatting, the hum of the computer, wind in the trees...

- Focus your awareness on these sounds and really listen to them. You might want to set a timer for how long you're going to do this exercise for, as it will help you, at first, to stay tuned.

- Don't attach any thought to the sounds. Just observe them.

Mindfulness gives the mind the clarity in which things can be seen 'as they really are'; it develops the ability to concentrate on an object for long enough to investigate it properly ... In these ways, then, calm 'tunes' the mind, making it a more adequate instrument for knowledge and insight.

www.mindfulnessinschools.org

" One in five people have dandruff. One in four people have mental health problems. I've had both. "

RUBY WAX

Most people can relate to depression somewhere on its vast scale. A low mood can bring back memories and thoughts from the past, and make us worry about the future. Mindfulness helps prevent these negative thoughts escalating and teaches us to focus on the present moment, rather than get caught in a tangle of reliving the past or pre-living the future. A course in Mindfulness Based Cognitive Therapy can significantly help people with clinically diagnosed depression.

Trying too hard to solve a problem often makes things worse.

It can close down the mind and prevent you from thinking creatively, whilst driving you round in ever-decreasing and exhausting circles.

This is where mindfulness offers a break in that circuit. A reminder to come back to the here and now, take a few breaths and do something completely different. It will give you the space you need. Not unlike the old adage of 'sleeping on it' when there is a decision to make.

Let the mind work its powers without the interruption of random thoughts.

It's not surprising our thoughts become jumbled and our minds frayed with the constant babble of communication going on around us. Practising mindfulness ensures that we give some oxygen to our thoughts and a space for them to settle. Try to have a period of time every day for half an hour with no mobile, telephone, email, television or radio.

Mindfully idling.

When you're standing in a queue, sitting in traffic, waiting for a colleague, a friend or a delayed train to turn up – use the time to be present without impatience.

Practise being still and enjoying the opportunity to slow down your body and mind.

" If you can spend a perfectly useless afternoon in a perfectly useless manner, you have learned how to live. "

LIN YUTANG

"So when the challenges come, as they always do, make a habit to go within at once and focus as much as you can on the inner energy field of your body. This need not take long, just a few seconds. But you need to do it the moment that the challenge presents itself. Any delay will allow a conditioned mental-emotional reaction to arise and take you over."

ECKHART TOLLE

A mindful listening practice.

1. Switch off your telephone for these few moments.

2. Take a piece of relaxing, single instrument music that you like.

3. Find a comfortable position, such as lying on the floor or the sofa (or sitting if you're at the desk or on the train!).

4. With the first notes being played, take a calm and moderate intake of breath and let it out slowly and naturally.

5. Continue to listen to the music, really listening to it, whilst your breath does the rest.

Do this for 5–10 minutes and you will be fully revived.

Weather patterns.

Just as we watch clouds or weather patterns in the sky, the same awareness can be given to thought patterns. To make a habit of observing thoughts and feelings, instead of continually becoming immersed in them, is to look at them more objectively.

Stormy weather comes and goes, as do sunny days. It's up to us how we respond to our observations.

*" You can't stop the waves,
but you can learn to surf. "*

JON KABAT-ZINN

You can change your mind.

In a film for the BBC, Dr Michael Mosley researched the neuroscientific results of practising mindfulness. As a self-proclaimed pessimist he asserted that doing the seven-week course on Mindfulness and Cognitive-Bias Modification (CBM) made him more optimistic, less stressed and a better sleeper. He returned to Elaine Fox's laboratory in psychology and neuroscientific research after the course to check the before and after results of the tests. The results were extremely encouraging and backed up the change.

People who are prone to higher levels of pessimism and anxiety have more electrical activity in the right frontal cortex of their brain. Following the course in Mindfulness and CBM, the levels of electrical activity were significantly altered.

"Change your life today. Don't gamble on the future, act now, without delay."

SIMONE DE BEAUVOIR

" Everyone knows that training makes our body stronger, fitter and more flexible. Now, neuroscience research shows that mindfulness training cultivates the innate capacities of the mind to be present, to step out of automatic pilot and to create space so we can be clearer, calmer, more focused, more creative, even more compassionate. "

JOANNE O'MALLEY

**10 reasons to bring meditation
to schools:**

1. Reduce stress in the classroom.

2. Improve students' concentration.

3. Enhance focus.

4. Strengthen memory.

5. Develop harmony and improve relationships.

6. Introduce a lifelong method to
   reduce stress.

7. Create a quiet time during the day.

8. Recharge the students' minds.

9. Offer staff the time to experience
   relaxation.

10. Lower anxiety around exam time.

ADAM DACEY
www.meditationinschools.org

" The faculty of voluntarily bringing back a wandering attention over and over again, is the very root of judgement, character and will. An education which should improve this faculty would be the education par excellence. But it is easier to define this ideal than to give practical instructions for bringing it about. "

WILLIAM JAMES

A mindfulness exercise to do with children.

Ask the child to select an object to draw … Tell the child to draw a picture of their object. Remind them that the activity is not focused on their ability to draw … Then the child should spend time looking at the actual object, paying attention to smaller and smaller details. Then the child should draw the object again. Compare the drawings, and ask the child to identify the details missing from the first drawing that they remembered in the second … the second drawing will be more accurate and life-like. Ask the child what it was like to spend time really looking at the object that might otherwise have been something they never took time to notice.

DAVID FONTANA AND INGRID SLACK
Teaching Meditation to Children

An important note about teaching mindfulness to children is that the person teaching should be comfortable with the exercises prior to the teaching, and have practised mindfulness in general. We must practise what we teach ... it is not something you learn about at a seminar or read about and then pass along.

Gestalt International Study Center

" *The true aim of everyone who aspires to be a teacher should be, not to impart his own opinions, but to kindle minds.* "

FREDERICK W. ROBERTSON

At a business meeting or at home, surprise yourself and your family by choosing to sit in a different chair or at a different place than you usually do. It will alter your outlook – and those around you – by the shift in perspective.

" I never came upon any of my discoveries through the process of rational thinking. "

ALBERT EINSTEIN

(Be) **Mind**(ful) (of) **Your Head!**

The average adult head weighs between 8–12 pounds. The brain alone weighs about three pounds. This is a considerable weight for the neck and shoulders to support.

Be mindful of keeping your neck and shoulder muscles loose and supple. Practise unclenching your neck and releasing and 'lightening' your head, which will help keep your neck supple as well as relaxing and aiding brain function.

In other words, practise being 'lightheaded'.

Mindful.
Not mind full.

Another way of looking at a mind overcrowded with thoughts all half dealt with is to compare it with the desktop on your computer. When you have too many files and windows open, the computer starts to groan. Sometimes opening just one more file is the last straw and the computer crashes or shuts down. When you are next at your computer think about this and let it be a mindful way of keeping your thoughts tidy and avoid your mind from 'crashing'.

" *Many emotional disorders are characterized by a mind that gets high-jacked – usually from thoughts that they are trying to address or repair. Meditation allows an individual to simply watch the mind and still the mind allowing it to do what it does, and you are able then to choose to follow it or not, and move to more wiser ways.* "

DR. ZINDEL SEGAL

**A SIMPLE 10-STEP BEGINNER'S
GUIDE TO MEDITATION.**

1. Sit tall.

The most common and accessible
position for meditation is sitting. Sit
on the floor, in a chair or on a stool. If
you are seated on the floor it is often
most comfortable to sit cross-legged
on a cushion. Comfort is key. Now
imagine a thread extending from the
top of your head, pulling your back,
neck and head straight up towards the
ceiling in a straight line. Sit tall.

2. Relax your body.

Close your eyes and scan your body, relaxing each body part one at a time. Begin with your toes, feet, ankles, shins and continue to move up your entire body. Don't forget to relax your shoulders, neck, eyes, face, jaw and tongue which are all common areas for us to hold tension.

3. Be still and silent.

Now that you are sitting tall and relaxed, take a moment to be still. Just sit. Be aware of your surroundings, your body, the sounds around you. Don't react or attempt to change anything. Just be aware.

4. Breathe.

Turn your attention to your breath. Breathe silently, yet deeply. Engage your diaphragm and fill your lungs, but do not force your breath. Notice how your breath feels in your nose, throat, chest and stomach as it flows in and out.

5. Establish a mantra *(optional).*

A mantra is a sound, word or phrase that can be repeated throughout your meditation. Mantras can have spiritual, vibrational and transformative benefits, or they can simply provide a point of focus during meditation. They can be spoken aloud or silently to yourself. A simple and easy mantra for beginners is to silently say with each breath, I am breathing in, I am breathing out.

6. Calm your mind.

As you focus on your breath or mantra, your mind will begin to calm and become present. This does not mean that thoughts will cease to arise. As thoughts come to you, simply acknowledge them, set them aside, and return your attention to your breath or mantra. Don't dwell on your thoughts. Some days your mind will be busy and filled with inner chatter, other days it will remain calm and focused. Neither is good, nor bad.

7. When to end your practice.

There is no correct length of time to practise meditation, however when first beginning it is often easier to sit for shorter periods of time (5 to 10 minutes). As you become more comfortable with your practice, meditate longer. Set an alarm if you prefer to sit for a predetermined length of time. Another option is to decide on the number of breaths you will count before ending your practice. A mala (a row of beads) is a helpful tool to use when counting breaths.

8. How to end your practice.

When you are ready to end your practice, slowly bring your conscious attention back to your surroundings. Acknowledge your presence in the space around you. Gently wiggle your fingers and toes. Begin to move your hands, feet, arms and legs. Open your eyes. Move slowly and take your time getting up.

9. Practise often.

Consistency is more important than quantity. Meditating for 5 minutes every day will reward you with far greater benefits than meditating for two hours, one day a week.

10. Practise everywhere.

Most beginners find it easier to meditate in a quiet space at home, but as you become more comfortable, begin exploring new places to practise. Meditating outdoors in nature can be very peaceful, and taking the opportunity to meditate on the bus or in your office chair can be an excellent stress reliever.

Meditation is a simple, effective and convenient way to calm your busy mind, relax your body, become grounded and find inner peace amidst the chaos of day-to-day life. Begin meditating today and reap the rewards.

JASON BELLOWS
Stop and Breathe

Mindfully moving.

As well as going for a walk with the sole purpose of switching off your chattering thoughts, there is another type of mindful walk that brings some calm to the day.

Instead of thumping around your daily activities with heavy feet and banging cupboards and doors, try doing it all more gently, starting with the feet. Being 'light of feet' is a physical way of 'walking lighter' and it transmits positivity throughout the body. (It also improves posture.)

Being light on your feet makes you 'fleet-footed' and therefore nimbler and faster. So a good way of getting to the tube or your appointment on time.

A mindful tasting exercise.

1. Take a small piece of chocolate, a raisin or a toffee of some sort.

2. Centre yourself with a few breaths.

3. Put the treat in your mouth and keep it there without chewing or swallowing, but prolonging its presence in your mouth. Fully concentrate on the taste sensation and all the different characteristics as it moves around your tongue.

4. Be gently aware of your breathing so that the two are harmonious.

5. After the taste has dissolved, focus on your breath for a few moments before resuming your activities.

You will have had a brief time out and enhanced your taste buds.

A mindful smelling practice.

1. Take something that you like the smell of – something natural. It could be a melon, a flower, a sprig of jasmine or lavender.

2. Hold it under your nose and close your eyes.

3. Breathe in naturally, savouring the aroma.

4. Take 3–4 breaths this way, until your breath is at a good gentle pace and you can take in the smell with each breath.

Done regularly, this will not only bring you into the present moment and give you a few moments of pleasure and calm, it will also enhance your sense of smell.

A mindful touching practice.

1. Choose something specific that you like the feel of: for example a piece of wood, a leather bound book, a pebble, an orange or a piece of velvet.

2. Closing your eyes isn't essential but it enhances the sensuality.

3. Breathe in whilst you really connect with the object, feeling the different curves, the temperature, the smoothness or roughness or any other characteristics that your fingers come into contact with.

4. Continue to take a few mindful breaths at your own pace to enjoy the sensations and exercise your awareness of touch.

81

A mindful singing exercise.

'I can't sing' is the usual response to this. But you can, as long as you are lucky enough to have a voice.

1. Take a few breaths to centre yourself, clear your throat and drop your shoulders. Breathe in a natural intake of breath.

2. Simply sing through the sonic range: *doh re mi fa so la ti doh.*

3. It is fine to just begin with *doh re mi.* Lead up to the full scale.

4. Come back down the scale: *doh ti la so fa mi re doh.*

A few of these will not only relax you and strengthen your breathing but also exercise your voice – ready for mindful talking!

" This ancient Way of Mindfulness is as practisable today as it was 2,500 years ago. It is as applicable in the lands of the West as in the East; in the midst of life's turmoil as well as in the peace of the monk's cell. "

NYANAPONIKA THERA

Take a minute to focus.

- Look at the second hand of a clock and watch one minute go by.

- Your task is to focus your entire attention on your breathing, and nothing else, for the whole minute.

Try it now ... to get a sense of time.

" When you are courting a nice girl an hour seems like a second. When you sit on a red-hot cinder a second seems like an hour. That's relativity. "

ALBERT EINSTEIN

Walk mindfully.

Think back to all of the places that you walked yesterday.

Perhaps to the car, to the bus stop, even from one room to another or up and down the stairs. In how many of those walks were you actually aware of the walking? And how many were done on autopilot?

Any walking activity is an opportunity to be mindful of the steps that you're taking and to disengage from internal chattering.

Live in the present moment.

Minding housework.

One of the many advantages of practising mindfulness is that it helps with the housework.

Whilst hoovering, making beds, cleaning the kitchen, washing-up etc, take the opportunity to switch off the brain and be attentive to what you're doing.

It's amazing how it turns a drudge into a pleasure.

Cultivating a plant for mindfulness.

Whether you're a landscape gardener or a buy-a-pot-of-herbs-from-the-supermarket kind of gardener, buy a plant to cultivate specifically for mindfulness.

Tend it every day, water it when necessary, turn it towards the light, keep its leaves clean if they're shiny and generally be attentive towards it.

This is your mindful plant and will remind you every time you look at it to be aware of living in the present moment. Tending the plant means not thinking about something else.

Packed lunches are commonplace, so why not packed breakfasts?

Instead of rushing out of the house without breakfast or picking up a coffee to gulp down at work, prepare a packed breakfast, with care and awareness, the night before.

Take your journey to work as usual, but allow an extra quarter of an hour to have your packed breakfast somewhere nearby (preferably outside), such as a park, favourite bench, garden square – just anywhere away from home or office preoccupations.

A moment to be mindful before the fast-paced day ahead.

" *When we are really honest with ourselves we must admit our lives are all that really belong to us. So it is how we use our lives that determines the kind of men we are.* "

CESAR CHAVEZ

Practise your breathing every day. That seems like a contradiction since your body will breathe for you. But breathing with your mind and senses as well brings you instantly in to the present.

Use the breath as an anchor for your attention and when you find yourself getting lost in internal chatter, stop the babble and come back to the breath. Feeling the wavelike movement as the abdomen rises with the inbreath and falls with the outbreath.

Don't take big breaths or change your breathing in any way, just watch it the way it is.

This is an instant re-energiser.

" You know that our breathing is the inhaling and exhaling of air. The organ that serves for this is the lungs that lie round the heart so that the air passing through them thereby envelops the heart. Thus breathing is a natural way to the heart. And so, having collected your mind within you, lead it into the channel of breathing through which air reaches the heart and, together with this inhaled air, force your mind to descend into the heart and to remain there. "

NICEPHORUS THE SOLITARY

Breathe – and – smile!

Be non-judgemental in your own thoughts, feelings and beliefs.

It is important sometimes to let things be, just as they are, and allow them to breathe without questioning or fixing.

" Some careful observers express the quite honest conviction that unless thought be raised to a far higher plane than hitherto, some great set-back to civilisation is inevitable. "

JAMES HARVEY ROBINSON

We think we cannot bring about world peace. But think of this: each person creating peace in themselves and with those around them can only, eventually, bring about peace in the world. Be mindful of practising peace wherever and whenever you can.

" Know yourself to improve yourself. "

AUGUSTE COMTE

Mindfulness helps you:

- To become familiar with the workings of your mind.

- To put you in touch with a different way of knowing yourself and the world.

- To notice small beauties and pleasures in the world around you instead of living in your head.

- To be kind to yourself instead of wishing things were different all the time, or driving yourself to meet impossible goals.

- To accept yourself as you are, rather than judging yourself all the time.

www.mbct.co.uk

" *Be happy in the moment, that's enough. Each moment is all we need, not more.* "

MOTHER TERESA

Various studies on the compassionate or mindfulness nature of leaders or supervisors have shown that their employees have a greater sense of well-being and higher performance – that is, they had less emotional exhaustion and a more contented sense of their own work-life balance. Mindfulness training can help you to become happier – and it can make you a better leader.

Michael Chaskalson, Mindfulness Works Ltd

The Difference between Concentration and Mindfulness

It is important to realise that there is a difference between mindfulness and concentration. Concentration helps you to focus your attention on one thing or another, and in this way it helps you to take command of what goes on in your mind. But mindfulness is another step beyond concentration. Mindfulness is a state of awareness. It is "presence" of mind.

www.themindfulword.org

" There can scarcely be a more noble capability of the mind than mindfulness, and its cultivation must surely be one of the more beneficial things we can do as human beings. "

ANDREW OLENDZKI

Reasons to be mindful

- People who are more mindful have greater awareness, understanding and acceptance of their emotions, and recover from bad moods more quickly.

- Mindfulness is correlated with emotional intelligence, which itself has been associated with good social skills, ability to cooperate and ability to see another person's perspective.

- People who are more mindful have higher, more stable self-esteem that is less dependent on external factors.

Michael Chaskalson, Mindfulness Works Ltd

Often one of the biggest challenges of childbirth is learning how to work with pain and anxiety. Learning how to use our minds to work with these challenges can make a huge difference in labour, birth and parenthood. The Mindfulness Based Childbirth and Parenting (MBCP) programme is an opportunity for learning about managing pain and stress and increasing 'availability' of attention for your baby by being in the present moment.

www.mbct.co.uk

Mindfulness is an aid to enhancing human potential by combining modern science with ancient wisdom.

The Oxford Mindfulness Centre

" *We shape clay into a pot, but it is the emptiness inside that holds whatever we want.* "

LAO TZU

Eastern meditation likens the pot to the body. So what we put into it (food) and what we fill our minds with (thoughts) is entirely up to us.

It is important, and helpful, to dwell on this when practising mindfulness.

" People are scared to empty their minds fearing that they will be engulfed by the void. What they don't realise is that their own mind is the void. "

HUANG-PO

- Only 10% of our stress is due to what happens.
- Whereas 90% is due to how we think about what happens.

Avoid stress and impatience by taking advantage of small waiting times:

- When the computer is slow at waking up.

- When the kettle seems to be taking ages to boil.

- When you are being kept on hold on the telephone.

- When waiting for a petrol pump to become free.

" Chance is always powerful. Let your hook be always cast; in the pool where you least expect it, there will be a fish. "

OVID

The 'instant tranquilliser'.

The Sigh Breath is a very simple breathing method for releasing tension in your chest, diaphragm and neck areas. It can be an excellent way of managing the symptoms of anxiety or panic, or a way of exercising before giving a presentation or an interview.

1. Inhale a moderate (rather than a very deep) breath through the nose.

2. Hold the breath for just a beat.

3. Allow the air to exhale slowly through the nose or mouth, whichever comes more naturally.

4. Allow the breaths to take their own natural rhythm until they become slower and shallower.

" If I had to limit my advice on healthier living to just one tip, it would be simply to learn how to breathe correctly. "

DR. ANDREW WEIL

Having recognised the health and cost benefits [of mindfulness therapy], some NHS trusts [in the UK] accept self-referrals, others accept referrals via GPs. The UK Mental Health Foundation, which has produced a list of some of the NHS-funded courses, estimates that as many as 30% of GPs now refer patients to mindfulness training.

MIA HANSSON
The Guardian

" If we can just let go and trust that things will work out the way they're supposed to, without trying to control the outcome, then we can begin to enjoy the moment more fully. The joy of the freedom it brings becomes more pleasurable than the experience itself. "

GOLDIE HAWN

Professor Lazarus [who was Professor of Psychology, Emeritus at UC Berkeley] emphasised that the way people cope with stress is crucial in their physical, social, and psychological well-being ... When coping is effective, stress is usually controlled; when coping is ineffective, stress mounts and can get out of control, leading to physiological disturbance, subjective distress, and impaired social functioning.

PROF. JOSEPH J. CAMPOS
University of California

When you can feel your stress levels rising:

- Take a slow, deep breath.

- Say 'stop' to yourself.

- Sometimes raising your hand in a 'halt' gesture can strengthen your intention to stop.

Practise mindfulness.
It's called practice for a reason. By practising awareness each day and exercising that muscle of attention, it will gradually become part of a new way of life.

Jon Kabat-Zinn tells people doing their 8 week programme of Mindfulness Based Stress Reduction (MBSR) that:

"You don't have to like it – you just have to do it!"

By the time you have been practicing every day for 8 weeks, you will have enough momentum and direct personal experience with the practice to keep going with it – for years or for life if you choose to.

JON KABAT-ZINN

" *The best way to capture moments is to pay attention. This is how we cultivate mindfulness. Mindfulness means being awake. It means knowing what you are doing.* "

JON KABAT-ZINN

Try bringing mindfulness into routine aspects of your daily life:

- When waking up in the morning.

- When brushing your teeth.

- When taking a shower.

- When drying your body.

- When getting dressed.

- When shopping.

- When travelling to work or to play.

There are endless possibilities of when to be alert and mindful.

Plant some watercress or beansprouts to extend your awareness and connection to the importance of taking care of our crops and food cycle.

Be mindful of the air that we breathe.

Keep it clean.

Imagine the benefits if we had a global
no-spray day.

If we can't make the whole world do it, let's
at least do it at home and at work.

One day a week. Use absolutely no chemicals.

Eating with awareness.

Take a piece of fruit that you can peel,
for example an orange.

Whilst you peel the piece of fruit reflect on
what brilliant packaging nature uses.

Be aware of all the processes that made this
possible for you to eat – the seed, the earth,
the weather, the crop pickers etc, all the way
into your hands.

Eat it slowly, knowing that it is adding to the
cycle of its life by improving yours.

Be reminded of all the cycles that we in turn
are part of to safeguard our environment and
keep our own footprints free from pollution.

Be mindful of everything that you are eating.

- Think about the source, the vitality, the nutrition and your digestion.

- Slow down your eating to avoid indigestion, tension in the stomach and overeating.

You will become more aware of what you are putting into your body and the sensations of tastes and textures will be heightened.

Managing your cravings.

Food plays such a complicated part in our lives that sometimes it is difficult to distinguish between what we need and what we want to eat. We tend to eat more of what we want to eat to the point it can simply become a craving, often with no nutritional value at all. So be aware of your cravings.

Ask yourself where they come from.

- What do you really want and are you going to get it from eating this particular food?

- Can you just eat a little of it?

- Are you addicted to it?

- Can you try letting go of it and just watch the craving as a thought or a feeling?

Applying mindfulness will gradually make it much easier to deal with these cravings.

When you're cooking fish you know that if you keep prodding the flesh it will start to fall apart and will not cook nicely. It is exactly the same with thoughts. Don't keep prodding them – be mindful of them and give them a chance to cook along on their own and surprise you with an outcome via your intuition. Trust the process.

Certain negative thought patterns can also be seen as cravings or addictions of no 'nutritional' value.

As with food cravings, can you just mindfully watch unwanted or negative feelings and thoughts?

Try to look at them objectively – see them as no longer 'my' thoughts and let them go.

Every time you do this you break the habit pattern of returning to them unnecessarily. You detonate the craving.

" We are what we think. All that we are arises with our thoughts. With our thoughts we make the world. "

JACK KORNFIELD

It is important to be mindful
of what we say...

" Wise men talk because they have something to say; fools, because they have to say something. "

PLATO

" In the end, just three things matter:
How well we have lived
How well we have loved
How well we have learned to let go. "

JACK KORNFIELD

Remember the advice of 'take a deep breath'? It remains one of the most instant mood changers and calming exercises. It's free, it's instantly available and it gets oxygen to your brain.

" *Carried away by our worries, we're unable to live fully and happily in the present. Deep down, we believe we can't really be happy just yet—that we still have a few more boxes to be checked off before we can really enjoy life. We speculate, dream, strategise, and plan for these 'conditions of happiness' we want to have in the future; and we continually chase after that future, even while we sleep. We may have fears about the future because we don't know how it's going to turn out, and these worries and anxieties keep us from enjoying being here now.* "

THICH NHAT HANH

The breath breathes itself. If it was up to us to remember to breathe, we'd have forgotten long ago ... the breath reminds us that at the core of our being, something is happening that depends very little on who we are or what we want to achieve. The breath provides a natural, gently moving target to focus on in your meditation; it grounds you in the here and now. You cannot take a breath for 5 minutes ago, or for 5 minutes' time. You can only take a breath for now.

PROF. MARK WILLIAMS AND DR. DANNY PENMAN
Mindfulness: A practical guide to finding peace in a frantic world

Learn to breathe again.

Learning to breathe properly is easy and will reward you with immediate results. Simply follow these 7 easy steps...

1. Stand or sit comfortably with a straight spine.

2. Relax your shoulders and place your hands on your lap or at your side.

3. Exhale completely, drawing the diaphragm in and up.

4. Slowly inhale through your nose by contracting your diaphragm out and down. Your belly should rise, followed by your mid-chest and finally your upper-chest as air fills your lungs.

5. Pause.

6. Slowly exhale through your nose while drawing your diaphragm in and up.

7. Repeat this process 3 times, taking consecutively fuller breaths with each inhale.

Congratulations, you've just taken 3 deep breaths! Many people have not taken the time to breathe this deeply since childhood.

www.stopandbreathe.com

By concentrating on the moment we're in, the worries of the past and the anxieties of the future dissipate.

" *The habit of ignoring our present moments in favour of others yet to come leads directly to a pervasive lack of awareness of the web of life ... and understanding of our own mind and how it influences our perceptions and our actions ... Religion has traditionally been the domain of such fundamental inquiries within a spiritual framework, but mindfulness has little to do with religion, except in the most fundamental meaning of the word, as an attempt to appreciate the deep mystery of being alive and to acknowledge being vitally connected to all that exists.* "

JON KABAT-ZINN

Do not miss experiencing the moment by always viewing the world through the lens of a camera. How many times have you witnessed a spectacular view and experienced the moment secondhand? It's good to take pictures, to have reminders of special occasions or people, but it can too easily become a substitute for being fully present in that moment or retaining it in the mind's eye. If it's all about capturing a moment in order to look at it in the future – it is to miss experiencing the moment itself.

" 'Ain't you thinkin' what's it gonna be like when we get there? Ain't you scared it won't be nice like we thought?'

'No', she said quickly. 'No, I ain't. You can't do that. I can't do that. It's too much – livin' too many lives. Up ahead they's a thousan' lives we might live, but when it comes, it'll on'y be one.' "

JOHN STEINBECK
The Grapes of Wrath

Focus on the now.

Stop waiting for life to happen!

Stop waiting for a better moment than the one you have had in the past or are hoping for in future.

Step into the present.

" Be here now. "

RAM DASS

Andy Puddicombe is a former Buddhist monk. He turned to secular mindfulness in order to demystify meditation, to make it accessible and relevant ... In a recent interview he stated that 6–8 weeks of practising a minimum of 10 minutes of mindfulness on a daily basis is enough to see significant and positive changes. Like any discipline – losing weight, getting fit, learning a musical instrument – there has to be a commitment.

Get Some Headspace App

" Mindfulness means non-judgemental awareness. A direct knowing of what is going on inside and outside ourselves, moment by moment. "

PROFESSOR MARK WILLIAMS

To help fit the practice of mindfulness in with your busy daily life and to have a method to hand at all times, download a mindfulness app for your smart phone, tablet or laptop.

" Mindfulness Based Cognitive Therapy brings together people who are in the same mental state in a compassionate, comfortable setting. Together they witness that they are not alone and that others are going through the same thoughts and feelings. "

DR. ZINDEL SEGAL

Why not start a mindfulness group of your own with a few friends?

Use an 8-week course such as the one outlined in Professor Mark Williams and Danny Penman's book *Mindfulness*, or one of several courses found online.

Having like-minded companions on the shared mindfulness journey is helpful in encouraging each other and helping each other practise until mindfulness becomes second nature.

" How often – even before we began – have we declared a task 'impossible'? And how often have we construed a picture of ourselves as being inadequate? ... A great deal depends upon the thought patterns we choose and on the persistence with which we affirm them. "

PIERO FERRUCCI

Thoughts are not facts.

" The life that is not examined is not worth living. "

PLATO

" *The value of life lies not in the length of days, but in the use we make of them. Whether you find satisfaction in life depends not on your tale of years, but on your will.*"

MICHEL DE MONTAIGNE

Happiness comes from kindness.

Happiness cannot exist whilst expressing hatred or anger.

Practise mindfulness to avoid negative and harmful emotions.

The problem of unhappiness.

By telling ourselves that we wish we were happier, we tend to focus on the gap between how we actually feel and how we want to feel. We are comparing something that we are thinking now with something abstract.

The mind then sees the gap as something to be solved. This can be disastrous when it comes to emotions because of the interconnection between our thoughts, emotions and bodily sensations. They all feed into each other and, left unchecked, can drive our thinking in distressing directions.

PROF. MARK WILLIAMS AND DR. DANNY PENMAN
Mindfulness: A practical guide to finding peace in a frantic world

" *Everyone thinks of changing the world, but no one thinks of changing himself.*"

LEO TOLSTOY

As well as practising mindfulness in daily life, it can be helpful to set aside time for a more formal mindfulness practice.

Several practices can help create a new awareness of body sensations, thoughts and feelings. They include:

Meditation – participants sit silently and pay attention to the sensations of breathing or other regions of the body, bringing the attention back whenever the mind wanders.

Yoga – participants often move through a series of postures that stretch and flex the body, with emphasis on awareness of the breath.

Tai-chi – participants perform a series of slow movements, with emphasis on awareness of breathing.

NHS, UK

Be mindful of the contact your body is making with whatever it is touching – your feet connecting to the ground, your back against the chair or lying on a bed or floor.

" What lies behind us and what lies before us are tiny matters, compared to what lies within us. "

RALPH WALDO EMERSON

To meditate you don't have to sit cross-legged on the floor.

However, many people who practise meditation frequently or for longer periods of time often do tend to sit in the contemplative cross-legged seated position. But to meditate is simply to contemplate.

Mindfulness meditation can be practised anywhere, in any position – as long as the mind is brought to the present moment – to be aware, be alert, be non-judgemental towards ourselves and towards others.

" *Meditation means to be constantly extricating yourself from the clinging mind.* "

RAM DASS

Choose a mindfulness cue.

For this excercise, you need to focus your attention on your breathing whenever a specific cue occurs. You could choose the phone ringing, the ping of an email, a siren or whatever works for you.

Then whenever you hear your cue you promptly bring your attention into the present moment and stay focused on your breath.

The objective is to have different random cues that will help to bring you out of 'autopilot' thinking and connect you with your breath and the present moment.

Do you need so much stuff?

- Be mindful of what you keep and store away.

- Clearing out your cupboards will help to clear out your mind.

Say you are holding a heavy parcel with both hands and someone gives you another parcel to hold – you would have to put the parcel you're already holding down in order to accept the second parcel.

It is exactly the same principle with thoughts. You can only hold one at a time.

So instead of juggling thoughts (or parcels), deal with each one before tackling another.

Keep your mind (or hands) free and ready to accept any new thoughts.

" *The outward freedom that we shall attain will only be in exact proportion to the inward freedom to which we may have grown at a given moment. And if this is a correct view of freedom, our chief energy must be concentrated on achieving reform from within.* "

MAHATMA GANDHI

We know that it is important to be kind and compassionate to others.

But it is also important to be kind and compassionate to ourselves.

Start with a day in which you mindfully accept yourself just as you are – be kind, non-judgemental and compassionate towards yourself.

" We are all affecting the world every moment, whether we mean to or not. Our actions and states of mind matter, because we are so deeply interconnected with one another. "

RAM DASS

Be mindful of being reasonable in your dealings with others because, as Lin Yutang states...

" Only in a world of reasonable beings can we have peace and happiness. The Reasonable Age, if that should ever come about, will be the Age of Peace. It will be the age in which the Spirit of Reasonableness prevails. "

LIN YUTANG

Be aware that we don't always have to be 'in the moment', and to force mindfulness upon someone can be counter-productive! We also need time to plan, think about things that have happened etc. It's only when we get 'stuck' outside the moment for too long that we miss what's going on around us. And remember, the younger the child, the shorter the time. Even a few seconds of really being 'in the moment' (concentrating) is a good start.

www.actonpurpose.com.au

Relax your mind at breakfast.

At the weekends (or during the week if you are not doing a packed breakfast) eat your breakfast outside if the weather is nice. Whether you have a garden, a patio, a yard or even a balcony you will find your mind automatically relaxes.

Instead of your morning emails, newspaper or mobile (which all demand answers or thought reactions) you can contemplate the weather, the sky, the plants or even just what you're eating.

" The secret of health for both mind and body is not to mourn for the past, worry about the future, or anticipate troubles, but to live in the present moment wisely and earnestly. "

BUDDHA

Mindfully working.

Before starting on a project or work task, it can be helpful to do one of the breathing or relaxation exercises to clear the mind and focus on being aware. Even three to five minutes sitting at the desk are all that are needed. In the same way that athletes steady themselves before making the move.

There is a lot of talk about 'focus'. Another word that is equally important is 'purpose'. Be mindful of your purpose in whatever activity you are doing.

" *If you use your mind to try and understand reality, you will understand neither your mind nor reality. If you try and understand reality without using your mind, you will understand both your mind and reality.* "

BODHIDHARMA

At the end of the day.

When you're lying in bed at night, before going to sleep, spend a few moments going back over the day so that you can see how mindfulness has made your activities and encounters more complete.

Think of the people you met and talked to and the events and progression of the day. If your mind starts to wander off into other thoughts or worries, or thinking about what you have to do tomorrow, gently bring it back to the present to continue reviewing the day and the wavelike motion of your breathing.

You are custodian of your own day. See this exercise as preparing for tomorrow by having put today to bed.

You will be asleep very soon.

" *Mindfulness is simply being aware of what is happening right now without wishing it were different; enjoying the pleasant without holding on when it changes (which it will); being with the unpleasant without fearing it will always be this way (which it won't).* "

JAMES BARAZ

Mindfulness cues.

In Buddhist monasteries mindfulness bells are used regularly to remind people to come back to the present in case their minds have wandered into the past or worried into the future.

We can use the same mindfulness cues by using bells that are all around us.

With just three conscious breaths we can release the tensions in our body and mind and return to a cool and calm state of presence.

That's all it takes. Three unhurried breaths.

No rush.

Break the habit of going straight to your mobile phone to check for messages and emails when there are some waiting moments. You don't need to be on call and available 24 hours of the day.

When you are mindful, you become a relaxed witness to your inner life, and you are freed from being constantly affected by all your mental activity and by all your judgements about the world and everything that's taking place within it. 'Observation' is the key word here. You consciously observe your thoughts and feelings, rather than allowing yourself to swim around in them. The moment you become aware and conscious in this way, you are living in the moment, and not on autopilot.

At first this feels like you are creating a sense of space within yourself. With time and practice it opens up a whole new dimension of freedom, relaxation and stillness.

www.the-guided-meditation-site.com

Watching a young child when they are playing or absorbed in painting or some other activity is a true lesson in mindfulness. A baby beginning to find its toes to play with, or faces and pictures to respond to, is equally inspiring – a reminder of the uncomplicated pleasures of living in the moment.

*" The only journey is
the journey within. "*

RAINER MARIA RILKE

BIBLIOGRAPHY

Books mentioned in *The Little Book of Mindfulness*

Bunson, Matthew E., *Wisdom Teachings of the Dalai Lama* (Plume, 1997)

Freke, Timothy, *The Wisdom of Zen Masters* (Godsfield Press, 1999)

Hawn, Goldie, *A Lotus Grows in the Mud* (Bantam Press, 2005)

Kabat-Zinn, Jon, *Full Catastrophe Living: Using the wisdom of your body and mind to face stress, pain and illness* (Delta trade paperback, 2005)

Nhat Hanh, Thich, *Peace is Every Breath: A practice for our busy lives* (Rider, 2011)

Nhat Hanh, Thich, *Peace is Every Step: The path of mindfulness in everyday life* (Ebury Publishing, 1995)

Puddicombe, Andy, *Get Some Headspace: How mindfulness can change your life in ten minutes a day* (St. Martin's Griffen, 2012)

Tolle, Eckhart, *The Power of Now: A guide to spiritual enlightenment* (Hodder & Stoughton, 2001)

Tzu, Lao, *Tao Te Ching*

Williams, Mark, and Penman, Danny, *Mindfulness: A Practical Guide to Finding Peace in a Frantic World* (Piatkus, 2011)

Yutang, Lin, *The Importance of Living* (Heinemann, 1938)

Further Reading

Boccio, Frank Jude, *Mindfulness Yoga: The awakened union of breath, body and mind* (Wisdom Publications, 2004)

Crane, Rebecca, *Mindfulness-Based Cognitive Therapy* (Routledge, 2009)

Gunaratana, Bhante, *Mindfulness in Plain English* (Wisdom Publications, 1993)

Hawn, Goldie, with Holden, Wendy, *10 Mindful Minutes* (Piatkus, 2012)

Hewitt, James, *The Complete Yoga Book: The yoga of breathing, meditation and posture* (Rider, 1991)

Kabat-Zinn, Jon, *Wherever You Go, There You Are: Mindfulness meditation for everyday life* (Piatkus, 2004)

Mello, Anthony de, *Awareness* (Fount Paperbacks, 1990)

Wallace, B. Alan, *Mind in the Balance: Meditation in science, Buddhism and Christianity* (Columbia University Press, 2009)

Wax, Ruby, *Sane New World: Taming the mind* (Hodder & Stoughton, 2013)

Willard, Christopher, *Child's Mind: Mindfulness Practices to Help Our Children Be More Focused, Calm and Relaxed* (Parallax Press, 2010)

Mindfulness Apps

www.mindapps.se

www.getsomeheadspace.com

Mindfulness Bell

Websites

www.franticworld.com

www.modernmeditation.ca/zindel-segal

http://oxfordmindfulness.org

www.nhs.uk/Conditions/stress-anxiety-depression/Pages/mindfulness.aspx

www.the-guided-meditation-site.com/mindfulness-meditation

www.mindfuleducation.org/mindfulnessforchildren.pdf

www.stopandbreathe.com

www.mbct.co.uk

www.mindfulword.org

www.mindfulness-works.com

www.meditationinschools.org

www.plumvillage.org/mindfulness-practice

www.thehawnfoundation.org/mindup/

www.mindandlife.org

www.pocketmindfulness.com/awesome-mindfulness-with-jon-kabat-zinn

http://tedxtalks.ted.com/video/Mindfulness-in-Schools-Richard;search%3mindfulness%20in%Schools

www.bemindful.co.uk

www.umassmed.edu/cfm

www.mindspace.org.uk

www.mindfulnessinschools.org

QUOTES ARE TAKEN FROM:

Albert Einstein was a theoretical physicist. He wrote many papers on the theory of relativity and received the Nobel Prize for Physics in 1921.

Andrew Olendzki is the executive director and senior scholar at the Barre Center for Buddhist Studies in Barre, Massachusetts.

Dr. Andrew Weil is a pioneer in holistic health. He is director of the Arizona Centre for Integrative Medicine.

Bodhidharma was an Indian Buddhist monk in the 5th/6th century and is largely considered to be the father of Zen Buddhism.

Buddha is the founder and original teacher of Buddhism.

Carl Jung was a revolutionary psychiatrist and psychotherapist. He is best known for having founded analytical psychology.

Cesar Chavez was an American farm worker and civil rights activist.

Dr. Danny Penman is the co-author (with Professor Mark Williams) of *Mindfulness: Finding peace in a frantic world*.

Eckhart Tolle is a spiritual writer and author of *The Power of Now*.

Frederick W. Robertson was an Anglican clergyman who showed exceptional oratory and psychological insight in his sermons.

Goldie Hawn is an American actress, film director and producer. She founded and now funds The Hawn Foundation, which teaches mindfulness training to children.

Huang-Po was an influential Chinese Zen Master in the 9th century.

Howard Thurman was an influential African American author and civil rights leader, as well as a well known philosopher and theologian.

Jack Kornfield is one of the leading Buddhist teachers in America, having practised Buddhism for over 40 years. He was extremely influential in introducing mindfulness to the West.

James Baraz is a teacher of meditation.

James Harvey Robinson was an American historian and the author of *The Mind in the Making*.

Joanne O'Malley is a mindfulness writer.

John Steinbeck was an American writer who received the Nobel Prize for Literature in 1962. He won a Pulitzer Prize for *The Grapes of Wrath*.

Jon Kabat-Zinn is the founding director of the Stress Reduction Clinic and the Centre for Mindfulness in Medicine, Health Care and Society at the University of Massachusetts medical school.

Lao Tzu was a philosopher of ancient China and author of *Tao Te Ching*.

Lin Yutang was a Chinese writer, translator, linguist and inventor.

Mahatma Gandhi was the leader of the Indian nationalist movement against British rule in India. His method of only using non-violent protest to achieve political and social progress has been hugely influential and he inspired later movements to use the same means.

Professor Mark Williams is Professor of Clinical Psychology and Welcome Trust Principal Research Fellow at the University of Oxford. He co-developed Mindfulness-based Cognitive Therapy (MBCT) and is Director of the Oxford Mindfulness Centre.

Michel de Montaigne was an influential writer of the French Renaissance, philosopher and well known for his work *Essais*.

Mother Teresa was an Indian Roman Catholic Religious Sister. She founded the Missionaries of Charity, a Roman Catholic religious congregation. She was the recipient of the 1979 Nobel Peace Prize.

Nicephorus the Solitary was a monk in the 13th century.

Nyanaponika Thera was a German-born Theravada monk and a teacher of Western Buddhist leaders.

Ovid was a Roman poet whose work strongly influenced more recent European art and literature.

Piero Ferrucci is an Italian psychotherapist, philosopher and author.

Pierre Teilhard de Chardin was a French Jesuit, a geologist and palaeontologist and the well known author of *The Divine Milieu*.

Plato was a philosopher and writer in Classical Greece – the student of Socrates and the mentor of Aristotle. Plato helped to lay the foundations of Western philosophy and science.

Rainer Maria Rilke was an Austrian novelist and poet who typically focused on themes of anxiety and isolation in his writing.

Ralph Waldo Emerson was an American preacher, philosopher, lecturer and poet, and the leader of the Transcendentalist movement.

Ram Dass is a well-known and highly regarded American spiritual teacher and author of the best-selling book *Be Here Now*.

Ruby Wax is an American comedian and author of *Sane New World*.

Rumi was a 13th-century poet and theologian who still maintains a great spiritual legacy.

Simone de Beauvoir was a French writer, intellectual and existentialist philosopher.

Steve Jobs was an American entrepreneur and inventor, who was the co-founder, chairman and CEO of Apple Inc.

Thich Nhat Hanh is a Zen Buddhist monk, author and one of the leading spiritual teachers.

William James was an American philosopher and psychologist, who was interested in the balance between the disciplines of physiology, psychology and philosophy.

W.H. Murray was a Scottish mountaineer, writer and soldier.

Dr. Zindel Segal is a cognitive psychologist, pioneer in the emerging field of mindfulness-based psychotherapy, specialist on depression and one of the founders of Mindfulness-based Cognitive Therapy (MBCT).

PAGE REFERENCES

Page 4: http://oxfordmindfulness.org

Page 12: www.mindfulnessinschools.org

Page 18: www.mbct.co.uk

Page 20: www.mbct.co.uk

Page 33: www.themindfulword.org/2012/mbsr-mindfulness-based-stress-reduction

Page 41: Williams, Mark, and Penman, Danny, *Mindfulness: A practical guide to finding peace in a frantic world* (Piatkus, 2011)

Page 43: www.mindfulnessinschools.org

Page 49: Yutang, Lin, *The Importance of Living* (William Heinemann Ltd, 1938)

Page 50: Tolle, Eckhart, *The Power of Now* (Hodder & Stoughton, 2001)

Page 56: http://mindfulnessatwork.ie

Page 57: www.meditationinschools.org/

Page 59: Fontana, David, and Slack, Ingrid, *Teaching Meditation to Children* (Element Books Ltd, 1997)

Page 60: www.gisc.org www.gisc.org/gestaltreview/documents/TeachingMindfulnesstoChildren.pdf

Page 61: *Great Teachers Change the World* (Pearson Education Ltd, 2006. http://www.pearsonlongman.com/great-teachers/pdfs/01-GT-change-the-world.pdf)

Page 67: www.modernmeditation.ca/zindel-segal/

Pages 68–77: http://stopandbreathe.com/2011/03/04/meditation-101-a-10-step-beginners-guide/

Page 83: www.mindfulnet.org/Mindfulness_in_Schools_Burnett_2009.pdf

Page 99: www.mbct.co.uk

Page 101: www.mindfulness-works.com

Page 102: www.themindfulword.org

Page 104: www.mindfulness-works.com

Page 105: www.mbct.co.uk

Page 106: http://oxfordmindfulness.org

Page 114: Hansson, Mia, *NHS Recognises that Mindfulness Meditation is Good for Depression*, The Guardian (26th February 2013 - reproduced with permission)

Page 115: Hawn, Goldie, *A Lotus Grows in the Mud* (Bantam Press, 2005)

Page 116: http://senate.universityofcalifornia.edu/inmemoriam/richardlazarus.html

Page 119: Kabat-Zinn, Jon, *Full Catastrophe Living* (Delta trade paperback, 2005)

Page 132: http://www.goodreads.com/quotes/tag/mindfulness

Page 134: Nhat Hanh, Thich, *Peace Is Every Breath* (Rider, 2011)

Page 135: Williams, Mark, and Penman, Danny, *Mindfulness: A practical guide to finding peace in a frantic world* (Piatkus, 2011)

Page 136–137: www.stopandbreathe.com

Page 141: Steinbeck, John, *The Grapes of Wrath* (Penguin Classics, 2000)

Page 144: Puddicombe, Andy, *Get Some Headspace App* (http://www.getsomeheadspace.com/shop/headspace-meditation-app.aspx)

Page 145: www.nhs.uk/Conditions/stress-anxiety-depression/Pages/mindfulness.aspx

Page 147: www.modernmeditation.ca/zindel-segal

Page 152: Bunson, Matthew E., *Wisdom Teachings of the Dalai Lama* (Plume, 1997)

Page 155: Williams, Mark, and Penman, Danny, *Mindfulness: A practical guide to finding peace in a frantic world* (Piatkus, 2011)

Page 157: www.nhs.uk/Conditions/stress-anxiety-depression/Pages/mindfulness.aspx

Page 169: Yutang, Lin, *The Importance of Living* (William Heinemann Ltd, 1938)

Page 170: www.actonpurpose.com.au © T & S Bowden

Page 180–181: www.the-guided-meditation-site.com

Editorial director Anne Furniss
Creative director Helen Lewis
Editor Louise McKeever
Assistant editor Romilly Morgan
Designers Emily Lapworth, Nicola Ellis
Production director Vincent Smith
Production controller Aysun Hughes

First published in 2013 by Quadrille,
an imprint of Hardie Grant Publishing

Quadrille
52-54 Southwark Street
London SE1 1UN
quadrille.com

Reprinted in 2013, 2014 (eight times), 2015 (twice), 2016 (twice),
2017 (three times), 2018 (thrice)
28 27 26 25 24 23 22 21

British Library Cataloguing-in-Publication Data
A catalogue record for this book is available from the British Library.

ISBN: 978 1 84949 420 5

Printed in China